This book is dedicated to all those people who think that they are losers in this cruel society of ours.
No, you are in fact, the winners!

-"The Don"
June, 2020

CONTENTS

1: Troubled Mind #2
2: Fornicationism
3: Masters of Destruction
4: Dance Me to the End of Death
(with regards L. Cohen)
5: Dark Side of the Earth
(The Pinkest of Floyd)
6: No Regrets
(Non, je ne Regrette Rien)
7: I'm a Loser
8: Making Ragu
(like a "real" Italian Mamma)
9: I'm Not Beautiful Enough
10: Sexy Beast
11: What Do You Want from Me?
12: I'm Still Standing
13: Words Have Power
14: Peter Kelly is Dead!
15: Ass High
(school is a battlefield)
16: A New Society
(Una Nuova Società)
17: Buffalo Boys
18: The Turing Test
19: The Myth of Sisyphus
(Le Mythe de Sisyphe)
20: Never Trust the People
21: People Have the Power
(Omines enim Potestas)
22: Two Worlds
(Me & Society)
23: Uranium
(the Friendly Element)

CONTENTS

24: Opinions
(des avis)
25: Needy & Greedy
26: I Lo♥e Capitalism
27: I Am A Hypocrite
27: I Want to Die with a Hard-On
(Just Like Billy Snedden)
28: Talking in Your Sleep
29: Silence is Not Golden
30: Sex Words
(parole sessuali)
31: Alice's Restaurant (Reopened)
32: Mindless
(less is better, less is more)
33: Mining Companies Care
(Oh, yes, they do, really!)
34: This Land is Your Land
(Reconciliation)
35: The Masturbation Game
(Guess the Gender)
36: World Environment Day
(6th June)
37: Taking it to the Streets
38: Recurring Dream
39: Respect
40: Metamorphosis
41: Yes, That's Me Babe
(That's Me You're Looking for Babe)
42: Police Brutality
43: Be Weird
(don't be NORMAL)
44: "The Don" Will Fuck You
(& educate you at the same time)
45: Living in a Fantasy World
46: Violence
47: History Repeats
48: The White Devil
49: Power to the People
(with thanks to J. Lennon)
50: Fuck the Patriarchy!
(with thanks to M. Pringle)

Acknowledgement of Land & of the Traditional Owners of this Land

I would like to acknowledge the Gadigal people of the Eora Nation, upon whose stolen land I stand today.

I recognise that this land was never terra nullius — the land belonging to these peoples was never ceded, given up, bought or sold.

I would like to pay my respects to Aboriginal Elders past, present and emerging, and I extend this acknowledgement to all Aboriginal and Torres Strait Islander people.

Dark History:

This Continent of Australia was claimed by the British Empire in 1770 by Captain James Cook.
His first action was to shoot an aboriginal dead from his ship, the "Endeavour".
The aboriginals had lined up on the shore watching this spectacle unfolding before their very eyes.

120,000 years of continuous culture & civilisation would end that day.
In an instant, the universe changed for these people.
For they were defined not to be people at all.
They were defined as uncivilised creatures.
To be used as slaves.

The British colonised Australia in 1788, with the arrival of Captain Arthur Philip & the 12 ships full of convicts that made up "The First Fleet".
They landed on the 26th January, which is celebrated as "Australia Day".
First Nation Peoples call it "Invasion Day".

There existed between 250-700 nations before the "White Man" arrived.
There were between 300,000 and 1,000,000 aboriginals living in Australia at the time.

In the last 250 years, First Nation Peoples have endured incredible suffering at the hands of the "White Man".

They have endured enormous cruelty at the hands of their oppressors.
Removed by force from their traditional land.
Suffered from introduced diseases they never had before.
Forced to assimilate into white culture & lose their own.
Forced into slavery.
Women were raped.
Their children were forcibly removed from their mothers & families.
They were later to become known as the "Stolen Generation".
The desecration & destruction of sacred & religious sites.
Addiction to alcohol introduced by the "White Devil".
Forcibly repatriated in Aboriginal settlements far away from their traditional lands.

First Nation Peoples did not have any rights in their own country.
In fact, this was no longer their country.
It had been stolen from them.
They didn't get to vote and until 1967.
They are still not recognised in the Australian Constitution.
No treaty has ever been signed between First Nation Peoples & The British occupiers.

These injustices have still not been resolved to this very day.

"The Don"
August, 2020

Foreword

There was a tale I once heard of an old man who lived in an apartment block in Glebe. I went to view the apartment in his block but unfortunately, it didn't have a car space for me, so the real estate agent said "There's an old guy that lives here who doesn't use his car space, I can work something out and maybe he'll let you use it." What I didn't know at the time, was that he was talking about not just an old man, but a young at heart old man, an old man who, when I met him and realised he was the same old man in this tale, would never let me use his fucking car space anyway! Prick.

The great thing about old men though - they tend to have incredible stories from the life they've led and 'The Don' is no exception to that.

When I first met Vito, he introduced me to his first book "My Life with Chickens and other stories" and I thought: Hey, this guy is batshit crazy! Then I read it. My perception never changed. This guy IS batshit crazy, but who doesn't love a bit of the old crazy!

Vito means "life-giver" and 'The Don' reads so true to his name. Full of wisdom beyond his very many years on this earth, 'The Don' will always bring a smile to your face (even if before the smile comes irritation, scepticism, horror and a big what the fuck just happened?).

Trust me, you'll still be laughing about it later!

Just do yourself a favour, start reading the goddamn thing. It will change your life. Who knows if it will be for better or worse? But you will never forget it!

Foreword by
"Jimmy" Fallon
June 2020

Troubled Mind #2

I'm concerned about the future of the Human Race.
Will we even be here tomorrow?
We are destroying the planet at an ever-increasing pace.
Global warming is changing the face of the planet.
Sea temperatures are rising higher each passing year.
Weather patterns are changing & becoming very unpredictable.
Days are getting hotter & hotter like never before.
Mega bushfires in Australia last for three months or more.
They destroy thousands of hectares of bushland & animals like never before.
Sea temperature is rising killing the coral in the Great Barrier Reef.
Pretty soon it'll be too late.
There'll be none of it left.

Storms & hurricanes causing flash flooding & massive devastation.
There is so much air pollution that we are choking & it's of our own making.
Animal species are becoming extinct every year.
Unable to cope with this rapidly changing environment that humans are creating.
We cutting down rainforests at unprecedented rate.
Destroying the habit of many animal species, such as orangutans & the great apes.
The Amazon, the mighty lungs of the planet, will not be breathing much longer.
It has been on fire started by greed & corruption & the lure of the all mighty dollar.
The youth of the world have seen the situation.

They have a spokesperson who is you & articulate but is ridiculed by the older generation.
"What the fuck does she know to speak about such matters!
Go back to school where you should be & don't waste your childhood on such important matters?"
The make fun of her & the way that she speaks.
They laugh at her & make fun of her looks.
"She is from Sweden, they all speak this way."
Her name is Greta Thumberg & she has something to say.
When will politicians, leaders of our great planet start listening & not putting her down?

She is not alone & her voice is not a cry in the wilderness.
There a millions of people who agree with her & will not go back to school & rest easy.

Trouble is a'brewing on this planet of ours.
Politicians must start acting soon or there will be a revolution.
Young people are fed up of being taken for a ride.
They are fed up of not being taken seriously & denied a voice to speak.
There will protests on the streets demanding to be heard.
There will be more days out of school to make their point be seen.
They know what the Future is & believe me it's not pretty.

The time has come to act if we want to save our planet.
If we don't the damage cause will be irreparable & irreversible.
It will be too late.
But I'm not so sure that these politicians even want to save our planet.
They are so deluded with their way of thinking that cannot see.
They are blind to what is happening & will never agree.

"This a natural state of events.
It's happened before.
It's not Human beings that are causing this situation!"

This is what they say.
This is their explanation.
They are old & fixed in their ways.
Unfortunately, I don't think they will ever change.
They will NEVER change.

So, this is why I have a troubled mind (again).

Troubled Mind #2

"The Don"
28.05.2020

Fornicationism

Fornicationism is the new "ism" to emerge this century.

There was:
Tribalism
Feudalism
Medievalism
Liberalism
Capitalism
Communism
Socialism.
Humanism
Futurism
Militarism
Totalitarianism
Nazism
Fascism
Nationalism

They all have their own particular political & social world views.
Fornicationism has too.

It advocates a "Fuck You" view.

Fuck Power
Fuck leaders
Fuck politicians
Fuck normalcy
Fuck conventions
Fuck traditions
Fuck obligations
Fuck money
Fuck profits

Fuck the Economy
Fuck bankers
Fuck economists
Fuck accountants
Fuck hate
Fuck wars
Fuck social norms
Fuck movie stars
Fuck fame
Fuck personalities
Fuck "reality" TV shows
Fuck advertising
Fuck advertisements
Fuck marketing
Fuck the market economy
Fuck the global economy
Fuck national borders
Fuck nationality
Fuck nationalities
Fuck fake news
Fuck churches
Fuck religion

Fornicationism is the new "ism"!
Some call it "Fuckism"!
It's the same thing!
Are you a "Fornicationist"?
Are you "Fuckist"?
Are you a "Fornicator"?
Are you a "Fucker"?

Join "The Fornicationist Movement" today.
You'll be so glad you did.

"The Don"
28.05.2020

Masters of Destruction

You Masters of Destruction,
You build to destroy.
You have no morality.
You have no principles.
You filled with hatred.
You want to destroy all that you hate.

You Masters of Destruction,
You are men of evil.
You do want you want.
You don't care of the consequences.
You create wars for your gain.
You only want power.

You Masters of Destruction,
You have greed in your eyes.
You have money as your God.
You have darkness in your heart.
You kill millions of innocent people.
You have blood on your hands.

You Masters of Destruction,
You seek to destroy.
You don't love beauty,
You don't value nature.
You don't value Love.
You have no soul.

You Masters of Destruction,
You create fear in the world.
You are to be feared.
You cannot be trusted.
You lie & deceive.
You are monsters, that can never be believed.

You Masters of Destruction,
You are demons & devils.
You are the creatures that populate our nightmares.
You are the terrorists that terrorise our minds.
You are the ghosts that haunt us at night.
You are the enemy within us, that we all have to fight.

You Masters of Destruction,
You are not our friends.
You are our enemies.
You are our destroyers.
You have no humanity.
You are the Devil's disciples, doing his dirty work.

You Masters of Destruction,
You will meet your judgement day.
You & your actions will be weighed.
You will be held accountable.
You will be sentenced for your crimes.
You will be sentenced to death for eternity, for being so heinous.

Masters of Destruction

"The Don"
28.05.2020

Dance Me to the End of Death
(with regards L. Cohen)

You took Suzanne down to the river.
You said so long Marianne,
It's time that we began,
To laugh & cry & laugh & cry about it all again.
And It pleased The Lord.
But you don't really care for music, do you?

You saw Jesus on the cross,
On a hill at Galilee.
Do you hate mankind for what they did to you?
Men will suffer,
Men will fight.
Even die for what is right.
If they only knew that we're only passing through.

But we're only passing through, passing through.
Sometimes happy, sometimes blue,
Glad that I ran into you.
Tell the people that we're only,
Passing through.

You lit a thin green candle,
To make her jealous of me.
You knew her well at the Chelsea Hotel.
She was giving you head on an unmade bed.
But you didn't go home with your hard on.
Otherwise, it'd only drive you insane.

You questioned,
Who by fire?
Who by water?
Who by sunshine?
Who by slow decay?
Who by his own hand?
Who by circumstance?
Who, shall I say, is calling?

First you took Manhattan,
And then you took Berlin.
Everybody knows, everybody knows,
That's just how it goes.
Everybody knows.
You saw the future & it's murder!

Your songs danced me to the end of death.
Your words had wings & made me fly into the heavens.
Your melodies sing in my head for ever & ever.
I will never stop singing them.
I am so grateful that you existed & left this world an everlasting song.
The Lord will be happy, L. Cohen.

"The Don"
28.05.2020

Dark Side of the Earth

(The Pinkest of Floyd)

Syd Barrett is waiting still.
Waiting to be called back into his band.
The band he formed with his best friend Roger.
They went to become one of the most influential musical groups in history.

But he could not handle the pressure & the fame.
He became addicted to heroin & lost his mind.
But he will always be the fifth member of the band.
He stands in the shadows where no one can see.
But he sings & plays his guitar as he always had done.
He never left, he was just forgotten.

But not good ol' Roger, who writes about you in every song.
Every word is about you, his long, lost friend.
How I wish, how I wish you were here, Syd.
We're two lost souls swimming in a fish bowl.
Year after year.
Going over the same old ground
And have found the same old fears
Wish you were here, with us Stu, once again.

You screamed that The Lunatics were in your head.
The Lunatics were in your head.
You thought you could tell.
Heaven from Hell?
Blue skies from pain?
A smile from a veil?
You thought you could tell.

Welcome my friend, welcome, to The Machine.
But shine on, you, crazy diamond.
Because we have become comfortably numb.
There's us, us, us, us.
And them, them, them, them
And after all we're just,
Ordinary men, men, men, men.

But With, with, with.
Without, out, out.
What the fuck is it all about, about, about?
Stu, you've fried your brain.
You have Brain Damage!
You are Brain Dead!

But the band must carry on.
The songs must be sung.
You will always be with us.
For we are a Band of Brothers
And together we stand & together we fall.

Actually, there is no dark side of the Earth.
It's all dark!

Dark Side of the Earth

"The Don"
27.04.2020

No Regrets
(Non, je ne Regrette Rien)

When your time has come.
When they ring the bell.
When the bell tolls for thee.
When the ref. blows his whistle.
When the final horn is blown.
When there is no more road to travel.
When you've reached the wall.
When you've reached the Abyss.
When your story has finished.
When you've run your last race.
When your ticker has stopped.
When your song is over.
When your song has been sung.
When you've had your last meal.
When your ship has come into port.
When your boat has finally docked.
When your eyes no longer open.
When you go to your eternal rest.
When your clock has stopped ticking.
When you've taken your last breath.
When you've run your last race.
When you've said your last goodbyes.
When you've put your house in order.
When you're asleep & never awaken.
When you dream & it never ends.
When you've reached the end of the rainbow.
When you've found your pot of gold.
When the fat Lady has sung.
When you're at the Pearly Gates.
When you've finally reached the End.
Make sure you have no regrets.

"The Don"
29.05.2020

I'm a Loser

I'm not rich.

I don't have a new flashy car.
I don't drive a Ferrari.
I don't have a yacht.
I don't have a Rolex watch.
I don't wear designer clothes.
I don't live in a posh area.
I don't have a huge house.
I don't have a 25m lap pool.
I don't own a horse.
I don't play polo.
I don't smoke cigars.
I don't go to whiskey bars.
I don't have a rural property.
I don't travel that much.
I don't have huge flat screen TV.
I don't own a plane.
I don't go on ski trips to Aspen.
I don't eat fancy food.
I don't have a lavish lifestyle.
I don't live in a gated community.
I don't have a gun.
I don't have security.
I don't have offshore bank accounts.
I don't get away without paying any tax.
I don't need highbrow lawyers to defend me.
I don't cheat the system.
I don't live for free.
I don't have my cake & eat it too.
I am not elitist.
I am not a snob.
I am a loser.

I am a loser in our society.
I am a loser but at least I feel free.
I am a loser but I can sleep well at night.
I am a loser with no debts chasing me.
I am a loser with no chains around my neck.
I am a loser put I'm not a prisoner of this society.
I am a loser with no money in my pocket.
I am a loser with holes in my shoes.
I am a loser but I stand upright & tall.
I am a loser but I don't feel small.
I am a loser but I have my head in the heavens.
I am a loser but that is the point.
I am a loser with a very full life.
I am a loser and I laugh at it all.
I am a loser because that's the way to be.
I am a loser because I wanna be free.
I'm a loser let me be.
I'm a loser in your society.

I'm a Loser

"The Don"
29.05.2020

Making Ragu
(like a "real" Italian Mamma)

Wanna be an Italian?
Wanna cook like "real" Italian mamma?
Wanna make the best ragu ever?
This is what to do.
Follow these simple steps.
It's mamma's recipe.
Don't be creative.
Simplicity is the best.
Never walk away.
No, that will never do.

Get an onion & some garlic.
Add lots of garlic.
Italians love garlic.
Drizzle some of the best, extra virgin, Italian, olive you can afford into a pan.
Cut the onion & garlic & put them in.
Fry them up until they are golden brown.
Don't overcook.
Don't burn them.
They won't taste good.
Never walk away.
No, that will never do.

Now, it's time to add the tomatoes.
A can of diced Italian tomatoes should suffice.
It should be bubbling away nicely.
Smelling like you're in an Italian trattoria.
Like in old Naples town.
Keep stirring.
Never walk away.
This is where mistakes are made.
Be careful, do not burn the ragu.
Don't walk away!
No, that won't do.

Next add some water.
Only a cup is needed.
Don't drown everything.
You're not making a soup.
Bring it to the boil.
Stirring as you do.
Never walk away.
No, that will never do.

Now, for the "piece de resistencé".
Add a dollop of tomato concentrate.
To intensify the ragu.
To give it that extra thickness.
Like mama used to do.
Only a spoonful is all you need.
Mix it in well.
Add salt & pepper to taste.
Even add some hot chillies.
If you can handle the heat.
Bring it to the boil.
Stirring as you do.
Never walk away.
No, that will never do.

Now, you've almost come to the end.
One last step is needed.
This is the step that most people omit.
This is the step that is most often neglected.
This is the step that cannot be skipped.
This is the step that will make your ragu really Italian.
This is the step that will make your ragu really taste like mamma's.
Back in ol' Napoli.
Never walk away.
No, that will never do.

Lower the heat.
Let it simmer.
Let it simmer for at least 2 hours.
The longer the better.
It's to do with separation of mixtures.
Between water & oil.
The oil should rise to the top.
Stirring occasionally.
Now, walk away.
Yes, that will do.

This is how to cook a ragu.
Like an Italian from the deep south of Italy.
This is a "Neapolitana" ragu.
From ol' Naples town in Calabria.
Home of the "Camora".
Up in the north they added meat.
This is because they were rich.
And could afford to.
But in the South we were poor.
We couldn't afford to eat meat.
But, our ragu was still the best.
Do you know why?
Because, simplicity is the best!

Making Ragu
(like a "real" Italian Mamma)

"The Don"
29.05.2020

I'm Not Beautiful Enough

I'm not tall enough.
I'm not skinny enough.
I'm not tall enough.
I'm not brown enough.
I'm not tanned enough.
I'm not blonde enough.
I'm not exotic enough.
I'm not cool enough.
I'm not funny enough.
I'm not smart enough.
I'm not beautiful enough.
I'm way too short.
I'm way too tall.
I'm way too fat.
I'm way too pale.
I'm way too tanned
I'm way too black.
I'm way too funny.
I'm way too smart.
I'm not beautiful enough.

I'm not too tall.
I'm not short.
I'm just the right height.
I'm just the right size.
I'm not too skinny.
I'm not too fat.
I'm just the right colour.
I'm not too dark.
I'm not too light.
I'm very exotic.
I'm very cool.
I'm not rich enough.
I'm not poor enough.
I'm just the right amount of smart.
I'm smart enough, when I wanna be.
In not too funny.

I'm funny enough to make people laugh.
I'm beautiful enough.

I'm beautiful enough inside of me.
I'm beautiful enough & that's all I can be.
I'm beautiful enough even if you don't see me.
I'm beautiful enough even if you don't agree.
I'm beautiful enough & I don't care what you think.
I'm beautiful enough & that's enough for me.

I'm Not Beautiful Enough

"The Don"
29.05.2020

Sexy Beast

I've got charisma to burn.
I've got nothing to Learn.
I can turn you on.
With my sweet song.
I'm the Italian stallion.
I'm also an ALIEN.
Come over let's feast.
I'm the Sexy Beast.

I make Lo♥e on the run.
I make Lo♥ing fun.
You've never anyone like me.
Come on over & see.
I taste very sweet!
I can think on my feet.
Come over let's feast.
I'm the Sexy Beast.

I'm as hot as fuck.
Come on, try your luck.
Wanna work out?
See what the fuss is about!
We can a have a meal.
To see how I feel.
Come over let's feast.
I'm the Sexy Beast.

I come with a warranty.
A complete guarantee.
You can get your money back.
You can even give me the sack.
If you're not completely satisfied.
You can even have me crucified.
Come over let's feast.
I'm the Sexy Beast.

I'm known as the "Sex Machine"
I'm the Lo♥er in you dream.
I have all the tricks.
I can send you for six.
I can even give you a surprise.
I'm the Devil in disguise.
Come over let's feast.
I'm the Sexy Beast.

I can make you sweat.
I'll make you forget.
About all the shit in your life.
And the fact you're are wife.
All your worries will disappear.
You can enjoy a moment without fear.
Come over let's feast.
I'm the Sexy Beast.

Do you like gelato.
Come on over & give me a go.
You've got nothing to lose.
Just, put downs, abuse & a very short fuse.
It'll be your time out of mind.
Who knows what you'll find?
It'll be your moment out of time.
Maybe, you haven't done the crime?
Come over & feast.
I'm your Sexy Beast.

"The Don",
30.05.2020

What Do You Want from Me?

I work 24/7.
This ain't no heaven.
I work as hard as I can.
I'm your biggest fan.
But that ain't enough.
You still treat me rough.
You claim I don't see.
What do want from me?

You say that "this is your life".
But we're still in a lot of stiff.
You say you work very hard.
But I'm no bucket of lard.
You say you wanna make this work out.
But you're not interested in what I'm about.
What do you want me to be!
What the fuck do want from me?

You say that we're in this together.
Partners in crime, forever & ever.
The "Dream Team" & the hitting the heights.
But you seem to forget about simple human rights.
You're going through a lot & that's very clear.
But you won't allow me to get very near.
You don't want to let me see.
What the fuck do want from me?

We'd better sort this out.
Find what this is all about.
Form a solution.
To all this confusion
I want my life back.
I want to get on back in track.
I wanna be free!
What the fuck do want from me?

"The Don"
30.05.2020

I'm Still Standing

I'm still standing.
Even after all these years.
I'm still standing.
Even through ball those tears
I'm still standing.
Have nowhere else to go.
I'm still standing.
Even if you told me so.
I'm still standing.
Through all the rain.
I'm still standing.
Through all that pain.
I'm still standing.
Even though it's not the End.
I'm still standing.
I will never bend.
I'm still standing.
We had so much fun.
I'm still standing.
Nowhere else to run.
I'm still standing.
Through thick & thin.
I'm still standing.
Even through all that sin.
I'm still standing.
I'm still on my feet.
I'm still standing.
Even though I've got be a seat.
I'm still standing.
Running my own race.
I'm still standing.
But I can't keep up the pace.
I'm still standing.
Better than I've ever been.
I'm still standing.
Through all the things I've seen.
I'm still standing.
With my feet on the ground.
I'm still standing.
Though I'm homeward bound.
I'm still standing.
Longer than I thought I would.
I'm still standing.
Yeah, yeah, yeah!

"The Don"
30.05.2020

Words Have Power

Be careful what you say.
Because words like bullets bark.
They will enter your skin.
They pierce your heart.
They will fester inside.
Like a rotting infection.
Growing ever bigger.
Each passing day.
Be careful what you say.
Because, words have power.

Just like a pen.
Which is mightier than the sword.
Words are more powerful.
More powerful than a gun.
You can be destroyed.
Just one word is all that it takes.
Aimed at the place.
Straight at the target.
Once inside it can never come out.
Be careful what you say.
Because, words have power.

Words can kill you quickly.
One word & you're Dead.
One word & you're on the ground.
One world can bend you over in agony.
One world can make your heart stop.
One word can blow your mind.
One word is all it takes.
One word can make you drop.
So, be careful what you say.
Because, words have power.

Words can kill you slowly.
Take a very long time.
You can piss off.
You don't even have to hang around.
But the dirty deed has been.
The seed has been sown.
Now, it's just a matter of time.
Before they start growing.
You can come & visit.
To see how they're doing.
Add some more words.
If you think they need improving.
So, be careful what you say.
Because, words have power.

But has to be the right word.
Be selective.
Cho0se carefully.
Take your time.
No need to rush.
The right word is all you will need.
To instantly kill.
So, be careful what you say.
Because, words have power.

But everyone knows this.
It's not a new thing.
Spells & incantations have always been around.
Hexes & jinxes & magical words.
Have been the backbone of religions.
Ever since the dawn of speech.
Magical words have existed.
That held great power.
Way beyond their reach.
In the sacred grounds of mysterious ceremonies & rituals.
Words with power have always been here.
So, be careful what you say.
Because, words have great power.

"The Don"
30.05.2020

Peter Kelly is Dead!

Peter Kelly was a good bloke.
He was deputy principal at Marrickville High School.
An inner west comprehensive school.
Typical of many others in the area.
It was a pretty tough place.
Kids from broken homes.
Damaged kids & he was their surrogate dad.
He looked after them like they were his own.

He was the guy who gave me employment.
He would ring me in the mornings.
And ask, "Can you work today?".
That's what he would say.
How could I say no?
Everyone wants to be needed.
So off I went, in my Sunday school best.
He would be sitting at his desk.
Sitting in his office.
He was a very important man.

He was a hardworking man.
A little bit overweight.
But who isn't?
He dreamed of cycling through South America.
"I'll have to train first.
Lose a bit of weight.
But I think I can do it", he used to say.
I hope he made it happen.

I still have his number stored in my phone.
I've never had the heart to delete it.
I just couldn't do it.
It just felt wrong.
Somehow, I felt it would be like, deleting the man.
Gone forever, even from my phone.
I still expect it to ring & hear his deep tones.
"Can you work today?".
That's what he'd say.

I often dream about him.
Giving me my daily allocation.
With his chubby, red smiling face.
Setting me off to my work for the day.
I didn't realise that he meant so much to me.
But that's always the case, isn't it?
You don't realise, until they're not there.
Until they're gone forever.
Never to return.
I guess I really miss him.
Even though we weren't really friends.

He died six months after he retired.
Someone told me in passing.
"Have you heard?
Peter Kelly is dead!"
I stopped in my tracks.
I was frozen to the ground.
That news was so shocking.
I could hardly breathe.
"What the FUCK!".
I said to myself.
"I can't believe it?
Peter Kelly is dead!"

I was so saddened.
Deep with such emotion.
I never thought I had for him.
I started to cry.
"No, I didn't know", I replied
"How did he die!", I asked.
"Apparently, from a heart attack.
He just keeled over".
I wanted to go to his funeral.
To say my last goodbye.
But I never got the chance.
So, I'll say it now.

In these few words.
I'll say my farewell.
To Peter Kelly.
I knew him, but not very well.
Peter Kelly is dead.
But he will never be forgotten.
Not for me anyway!

"The Don"
31.05.2020

Ass High

(school is a battlefield)

I got a promotion to Bass High.
I was the new Head Teacher Admin.
With my own office & my name on the door.
This was a good start, I thought.
But it went downhill from there.
I went from Heaven to Hell.
In one single day.
Getting there was an adventure in itself.
You had to drive through *"The Dead Zone"*,
"The Forbidden Zone" & *"The Place with No Name"*.

The first day there, I saw all these student's playing outside.
I asked, *"is it recess or something?"*
*"No, there's not enough teachers to cover these classes.
There is no one to look teach them, so they have to go outside!"*
It seemed to me that there were more students outside,
Then there were in the classrooms being taught.
This did not bode well for me.
For my stay in this Hell.

One of my jobs was to ring for relief teachers.
Asking them to work for a day.
To relieve another teacher,
That was sick or away.
To take over their classes & try to teach.
Just for a day.
But it wasn't easy to get some relief.
The word has gone out.
There was no one about.
Stay away from that school.
It's rough & tough.
You'll never make back alive.
You'll never make it through the day.

The first thing that catches your eye.
As you go past the facade of Bass High.
Someone had stolen the "B".
It had never been replaced.
It spoke so eloquently about the place.
What you were about to embrace.
"Forewarned is to be prepared" or so they say.
But no one could prepare you for this place.

The Principal was Phil Goodacre.
A really nice block.
But he was a civilised man.
Not a place for him here.
His weapons were kindness, civility & good will.
He had no hope in hell, in this place.
One time I sent a student to him for some discipline.
The student apologised for his misdemeanours & sins.
*"I very sorry Sir, I won't do it again.
I've learnt my lesson.
I'll behave from now on!"*

Armed with a note for his return.
He smashed every window & door.
Walking back to my classroom.
There are so many more stories I could tell.
Of the time I did my time.
Four years of living Hell.
On my last day as drove away.
I yelled as loud as I could.
"FREEDOM!"
I've never returned since.
I've never been back.
But I can never forget my time at ***"Ass High"***.

"The Don"
31.05.2020

A New Society

(Una Nuova Società)

Serenity
Serendipity.
Tranquility.
Positivity.
Universality.
Synchronicity.
Multiplicity.
Simplicity.
Spontaneity.
Commonality.
Superficiality.
Personality.
Alienanity.
integrity.
Intercity.
Intracity.
Biodegradability.
Livability.
Habitability.
Poverty.
Loyalty.
Curiosity
Luminosity
Plurality.
Subjectivity.
Sanity.
Sincerity.
Hospitality.
Spontaneity.
Locality.

Living in a Community.
With Spirituality.
And Humanity.
With Musicality.
It's not a Difficulty.
It's a Probability.
Without Negativity.
And only Positivity.
With no Nationality.
Complete Liberty.
Let's sign a treaty.
It's a possibility.
To make this a Certainty.
And add it to our Constitutionality.
We can create a new Mentality.
A New Society!

A New Society

(Una Nuova Società)

"The Don"
31.05.2020

Buffalo Boys

The Buffalo Boys have come out play.
It's so much fun to see them together again.
They should never be separated ever again.
Together, forever that's the way it should be.

The Buffalo Boys do everything together.
They are never apart.
They one & the same.
They share the same bed.
They eat the same food.
They wear the same clothes.
Hell, they even have the same wife.

The Buffalo Boys enjoy their own company.
They are always happy, frivolous & free.
They their own best friends.
They need nobody else.
They are twin brothers.
They have the same identity.

The Buffalo Boys have tried being apart.
It didn't go well.
It was like a part of them was missing.
When they were separated for a time.
Each of them being the lesser.
When they are apart.
But together they are one.
Complete & fulfilled.
One entity, one body & one mind.

The Buffalo Boys are an inspiration to me.
In fact, they're an inspiration to the whole world.
That, together we a stronger than being alone.
Together we are more powerful than be apart.
The unity of one being. that is mighty force.
That's what they've shown, those Buffalo Boys.

"The Don"
31.05.2020

The Turing Test

Can you pass the test?
Are you Human?
Are you intelligent?
Are you sentient?
Are you self-aware?
Are you living?
Are you conscious?
Are you awake?
Are you aware of yourself?
Are you aware of your own existence?
Are able to say, "I think therefore I am"?
Are you self- perceptive?
Are you cognitive?
Are you cognisant?
Are you living being?
Are you a machine?
Are you alive?
Are you up to it?
Are you ready to have a go?
Are you ready to risk it all?
Are you prepared to take a risk?
Are you ready to pass the test?
Are you ready to fail the test?
Are ready to find out what you are?
Are you ready to see if you're like all the rest?
Are you prepared to take The Test?
Are you ready to take The Test?
Are you prepared to take The Turing Test?
Are ready for the results?
Are ready for the results of The Turing Test?

"The Don"
01.06.2020

The Myth of Sisyphus

(Le Mythe de Sisyphe)

It's a question of intention.
It's a question of fact.
Does our life have meaning?
Or is it a useless, repetitive act?
This has been the quest for Humanity.
To answer this fundamental question.
Is it just a matter of Fate?
That there is nothing we can do about it.
That we are destined to do that what is planned.
Regardless of our intent.
That we are prisoners to our destiny.
No matter what.
That we have no choice in the matter.

Is this our situation?
To struggle for absolutely no gain?
To suffer needlessly?
And to do it, again & again?
To keep repeating the same old things?
Without any meaning or purpose?
To live a life of meaninglessness?
For our live to be a complete waste of time?

Is this our punishment?
For something that we've done?
An act so heinous.
So abominable.
That we are cursed to push the rock up the mountain.
Once at the top, to let it go.
Watch it roll back down to the bottom.
And then do it all again.
To this for an eternity?
Like poor old Sisyphus.
He was destined to do.
Maybe, it not a myth after all.
Maybe, it's TRUE!
Maybe this is our Reality?
It is actually, The Reality of Sisyphus.

"The Don"
01.05.2020

Never Trust the People

Never trust the people.
That's what my old man used to say.

Never trust the people.
They'll always let you down.

Never trust the people.
They will never hang around.

Never trust the people.
They only want to use you.

Never trust the people.
They only want to abuse you.

Never trust the people.
They cannot be trusted.

Never trust the people.
It's sad but it's true.

Never trust the people.
There's nothing you can do.

Never trust the people.
It's just the way things are.

Never trust the people.
It's the way of the world.

Never trust the people.
Even your family.

Never trust the people.
Never have any friends.

Never trust the people.
That's what my old man used to say.

Never trust the people.
My old man died alone.

"The Don"
02.06.2020

People Have the Power
(Omines enim Potestas)

Do people really have the power?
I'd like to believe that this is true.
It's supposed to be like this in democracy.
Although, I'm not so sure anymore.

Power lies in the hands of the people.
I'd like to think this is the case.
Although, I look around at the state of the world.
It definitely doesn't look this way.

People have the power.
That's wonderful thing.
However, society seems to controlled by only few.
The rich are the powerful.

The will of the People must be served.
The question is, "which people?"
The will of only these few, that have all the money.
It's sad but it's true.

Society is ruled by money.
Society is ruled by greed.
Society is governed by stupid men.
Society is not governed by all people.

People can go out into the streets.
People can protest & show their anger.
People can demonstrate as much as they like.
But nothing really matters.

These that have the Power.
Those very lucky few.
Never listen to what the people want.
You don't really expect them to.

These few, in the hands in which Power is concentrated.
These few men, in whose hands all Power is held.
These few greedy, selfish, psychos that have all the Power.
They will NEVER secede, to the Will of the People.

The never think they need to.
Power is not a sharing thing.
Once you have, you don't want to pass it around.
You want to keep for yourself & fuck everyone.

People have the Power.
That's a myth.
It's not the case at all.
It's a fairy tale, so you can go to sleep at night.

People do not have the Power.
The voice of the People is never heard.
The Will of the People is never served.
Don't you believe what you've been told or you've heard.

People do NOT have the Power.
It's sad but it's true.
You are delusional if you in this lie.
It's just perpetuated to keep the masses quiet.

People do NOT have the Power.

Omines enim Potestas
(People have the Power)

"The Don"
02.06.2020

Two Worlds
(Me & Society)

There are two worlds.
There is My World
And there is The World.
The two are inexplicably linked.

I live in two worlds.
My own world.
And the larger outside world outside of my reach.
This world is called Society.

Whatever happens in Society affects me.
Whatever I do in my little world affects society.
But not to the same degree.
My world is a small, tiny little world.

Society is a huge, big world.
I don't like society very much.
I don't agree with its values & priorities.
It's not where I want to live.

But this is the key.
Here is the rub.
I can create my own little world.
I can make how I like.

It's all up to me.
How I would like my little world to be.
It doesn't have to be like society.
I can make it the way I want to live.

This is beginning to make sense.
I beginning to feel free.
Free to create my own reality.
Free to be who I want to be.

I need society, that is true.
But I can create my own little world.
A world within another world.
A world that's built by me.

This is how I can be free.
This how can live in happiness.
This is how I can change society.
There are two worlds.

The two worlds are, Mine & Society.

"The Don"
02.06.2020

Uranium

(the Friendly Element)

Uranium is named after the planet Uranus.
At school, everyone made fun of Uranus.
For obvious reasons.
Especially boys!
Are we going to "your anus?"
It was hilarious.
For some reason boys like dicks and arse jokes.
Probably because they're funny!

Anyhow, I digress.
Uranium is a naturally radioactive element.
It was discovered in the late 18th century.
It was not considered very important at the time.
It was a bit of a novelty.
No one knew the power that it held hidden inside.
It was the sleeping Dragon.
Waiting to be awoken.

It was not until Albert Einsteen (Einstein,) came along.
(Einsteen to me, Einstein to you!).
With his equation that changed the world forever.
Emmc!
Marrying energy with matter, as one & the same.
Energy is Matter & Matter is Energy!
This is what it said.
Slow down Energy, it becomes Matter.
Speed up Matter it becomes Energy!

This was a mind explosion.
This was a new revelation.
This the beginning of a new era.
The era of the nuclear age.
Unlimited power was the dream.
This unlimited power was to destroy.
The age of massive destruction had begun.

It was 1942, Los Alamos, New Mexico, in the US of A.
It was called "The Manhattan Project".
It was top secret project.
Led by a German scientist called Robert Oppenheimer.
To make the first atomic bomb.
Power beyond human imagination.
This is what was created in those laboratories.

It was 8:00am, 6th of August 1945.
The Enola Grey, an American B52 bomber flew over a city in Japan.
In its belly was a cargo that was going to unleash unbelievable destruction.
Its name was "Little Boy", the first atomic bomb.
When it was dropped, the dragon was awoken.
The fire of the dragon obliterated a whole city.
That city was Hiroshima.
150,000 people were evaporated in an instant.
The gates of Hell had been opened.
Three days later another was dropped on Nagasaki
Another 80,000 people were evaporated in an instant.

Oppenheimer then uttered those infamous words.
That would become etched forever in history,
"I am become Death, the Destroyer of Worlds!"
No truer words have ever been spoken.
No sadder statement has ever been made.
He knew of his place in history was sealed.
He was the one that had awoken the dragon.
He was the man who had set it free into the world.
Once released, it could never be captured again.

It flies around ready, to unleash its deadly power.
And if we're not careful,
The annihilation of the whole Human Race.

"The Don",
02.06.2020

Opinions
(des avis)

Opinions are just opinions.
And all they'll ever be.
Everyone's got them.
They're cheap & free.
People are so easy to share them so readily.
In fact, sometimes they should let them out
They should keep caged up inside them.
And not let them run about.
Because once they are out into society.
They can run amok, cause havoc & get out of control.

Yes, you can have opinions.
No one can stop you of that.
But keep them to yourself
Don't let them roam about.
It's so damn easy to think your opinions are the best.
To FUCK everyone.
FUCK all the rest.
This is where the problem lies.
This is the nexus.
This is the heart.

Your opinions are no better than mine.
In fact, they could be far worse than mine & all of the rest.
See your opinions you have to depend on your values.
If your values are fucked.
I'm afraid to say, so are your opinions.
So, don't impose them on me.
Keep them to yourself.
In your own little world.
History will determine whether they are shit or not.

So, if you have to state your opinions out in society,
Always start by saying,
"These are just my opinions & they seem to work for me!
They are not the "Truth" & the only way to be!
My opinions of you don't define who you are.
Your opinions of me doesn't define who I am."

"The Don"
02.06.2020

Needy & Greedy

Don't be desperate.
Don't be craving.
Don't be wanting.
Don't be begging.
Don't be grovelling.
Don't be frothing.
Don't be leering
Don't be needy.
Don't be greedy.

It's not a good look to be so desperate.
It's not a good look to be so pathetic.
It's not a good look to go grovelling around.
It's not a good look to be bending the knee.
It's not a good look to be begging for Lo♥e.
It's not a good look to be greedy in Lo♥e.

Just be cool & let it flow freely.
That is the way that Lo♥e will come to thee.
Don't go chasing, let it come to you.
Have faith in yourself.
That's all you need to do.

This is what is attractive to me.
To see another person who is footloose & free.
To be able to dance through the Corridors of life.
Like a butterfly or a bee.
To float in the air like a gossamer in the wind.
This is a very attractive thing.

So, don't be tied down to the ground.
By earthly chains that are so heavy & strong.
These chains are called Needy & Greedy.
They keep you enchained & earthbound.
Cut them free & become unshackled.
From Needy & Greedy & off you will travel.

"The Don"
02.06.2020

I Love Capitalism

I love money.
I love capital.
I love profit.
I love materialism.
I love the stock market.
I love buying & selling shares.
I love accountants.
I love economists.
I love bankers.
I love banks.
I love companies.
I love multinational companies.
I love the World Bank.
I love the IMF.
I love borrowing money.
I love interest rates.
I love greed.
I love being rich.
I love buying beautiful things.
I love acquisition.
I love buying.
I love selling.
I love having a mortgage.
I love having a mortgage for the rest of my life.
I love having a credit card.
I love having a debit card.
I love having a VISA card.
I love being in debt.

I love working hard for little pay.
I love working long hours.
I love being exploited.
I love my working a shitty job.
I love having to grovel.
I love having to suck up to my boss.
I love being overworked.
I love being underpaid.
I love towing the line.
I love losing my individuality.
I love not being valued.
I love be expendable.
I love doing repetitive, menial tasks.
I love being treated like garbage.
I love being thrown out when I am past my "used by date".
I love being demeaned.
I love having no rights.
I love being treated like an object.
I love being dehumanised.
I love being stepped upon.
I love being trodden on.
I love being kicked around.
I love being thrown down.
I love being treated a disposable rag.
I love being spat on, shat on, pissed & kicked the guts.
I love Capitalism.

I just love money so much.
I just love Capitalism so much!

"The Don"
02.06.2020

I AM A HYPOCRITE

I am a hypocrite.
I am full of shit.
I can't be trusted one little bit.
I say one thing & do something else.
I will say anything to get my own way.

I am a hypocrite.
What I say is full of shit.
I can't be believed one little bit.
I can't be trusted one little bit.
Don't listen to me, I'm a creep.

I am a hypocrite.
I am so full of it.
I lie all the time.
I don't care about what I say.
I don't care what I do.

I am a hypocrite.
I have no morality.
I have no integrity.
I have no principles.
I have no scruples.

I am a hypocrite.
I take what I want.
I don't give a damn about anyone else.
I am not number one.
I say, "Fuck the rest"

I am a hypocrite.
I want everything for me.
I want everything for free.
I don't give a shit about society.
I don't give a fuck about humanity.

I am a hypocrite.
I am greedy & everything's for me.
I don't care for anybody else.
I only think for myself.
I want to win this race.

I am a hypocrite.
I don't care what you think of me.
I say, "Fuck you!".
I don't need anyone else.
I'm a loner, a "son of a gun".

I am a hypocrite.
I don't care one little bit.
I am a hypocrite.
I know I'm full of shit.
I am a hypocrite.
I speak lots & lots of "bullshit".
Because, I am a hypocrite.

I AM A HYPOCRITE

"The Don"
03.06.2020

I Want to Die with a Hard-On
(Just Like Billy Snedden)

Some want to have a steak for their last meal.
Some want to get stoned & be outta their minds.
Others want to drink a fine single malt whiskey.
I want to die with a hard-on (just like Billy Snedden).

Now, you probably don't know who Billy Snedden was.
He was a man of great stature, substance & style.
He almost rose to the pinnacle of power.
The highest office in the land, that of Leader of this country.

He was leader the Liberal Party in the 1980s.
When they were in opposition.
But what makes him so famous & a hero to me.
Was not what he did in life but how he took his last breath.

He was found dead in the Ritz-Carlton Hotel, Double Bay, Sydney.
Laying in bed the biggest hard-on anyone had ever seen.
Apparently, the cause of death was a cardiac arrest.
Whilst performing the holist of acts, that of "coitus interruptus".

He was found sprawled spread eagled on the bed.
His "shlong", standing massive, tall & resplendent.
At complete attention, frozen forever in time.
The evidence was all the scene of the crime.

He was fucking a sex worker at the time of his death.
He was having the time of his life.
How was he to know it was also his death.
In throws of ecstasy, he took his last breath.

His heart exploded at the same as his cock.
"Ride me big boy", she said, unaware of the situation inside her.
The look on his face was one of pure pleasure.
Little did she know it was also his "death mask".

The horror immediately seized her.
As she felt his life slip away beneath her.
Billy lay stiff as a board & so was his cock still inside her.
She freaked right out.

She had had many strange & weird strange situations.
But nothing like this had happened to her before.
No one had ever died while being fucked.
So, she quickly got her stuff & off she ducked.

So, this is the story of the death of the great Billy Snedden.
One of the greatest stories of death, ever to have happened.
Even his son said, "What a great way to go".
I want die with a hard-on, just like Billy Snedden!

I Want to Die with a Hard-On
(Just Like Billy Snedden)

"The Don"
03.06.2020

Talking in Your Sleep

You've got a lot to say.
You've got a lot on your mind.
There's not enough time during the day.
You have to say it at night.
You're talking in your sleep.

What's on your mind.
What are you thinking about?
You got things to say.
But you can't get them out.
That's why you're talking in your sleep.

You can't talk during the day.
You can't speak your mind.
No one will listen anyway.
There's not enough time.
So, you're talking in your sleep.

You don't even know it.
You not aware.
There are things on your mind.
You've got to say.
That's why, you're talking in your sleep.

These are important things.
These are unspoken truths.
You're not even aware of them.
They're deep inside you mind.
So, you're talking in your sleep.

They're in your subconscious.
They're deep underground.
They are the shadows lurking in your mind.
They only arise at night.
When you're talking in your sleep.

They're subterranean ghosts.
In the caverns of your mind.
They are held captive during the day.
They only come when you're asleep.
And you start talking in your sleep.

They are prisoners during the day.
They cannot see the light.
It's only late at night.
In the darkness, that they can be free.
And you're talking in your sleep.

Only somebody else can hear them.
If you're lucky to be sleeping with someone else.
They'll probably be awoken by your babblings.
Your incoherent shouts.
They'll elbow in your ribs.
"What the fuck?"
You were talking in your sleep.

"The Don"
04.06.2020

Silence is Not Golden

Don't hold your tongue.
Don't bite your lips.
Don't be quiet.
There things happening in the streets.
Now is not the time to be silent.
Now is not the time to be meek.
Come open your mouth & speak, speak.

Shout as loud as you can.
Shout it to the man.
Make it so loud.
That they can hear it in Hell.
Don't live in fear.
Don't regret you never opened your mouth.
Now's the time to take a stand.
So, get to your feet.
Open your mouth & speak, speak.

This is the time for you voice to be heart.
Now, is the two me to join the choir of Humanity.
Now, is the time, for your prays & your tears.
Now is the time to raise our voices after all these years.
Now is the time for the Heavens to hear.
The beautiful song of Humanity, so crystal & clear.
So, open your mouth & speak, speak.

Sing this beautiful song like you've never sung before.
Song with all your heart & then even some more.
Sing till you go red in your face.
From happiness, joy & this holy grace.
This is our church.
This is our religion.
This is the family of Humanity.
So resplendent & pure.
Now is the time to open your mouth & speak, speak.

"The Don"
04.06.2020

SEX WORDS

(parole sessuali)

Screw
Root
Boner
Tool
Muffpie
Felatio
Cunnilingus
Fornicate
Coitus Interruptus
Shlong
Shmedium
Shlort
Fanny
Pissflaps
Trouser snake.
Honey Pot
Snatch
Cunt
Cock
Prick
Dick
Richard Cranium
Dick Head
Arsehole
shithole
Rear Ender
Penis
Vagina
Masturbation
Wank
Jerk off
Spank the monkey
Boobs
Boobies
Tits
Titties
Butt
Butthole
Butthead

Jugs
Cow's Udders
Whore
Slut
Slag
Gigolo
Casanova
Two-timer
Missionary position
Doggy style
Knocked Up
Flagulate
Sadomassochist
Bondage
Auto Erotic Asphixiation
Eroticism
Lo♥e
Lo♥er

SEX WORDS
(parole sessuali)

"The Don"
04.06.2020

Alice's Restaurant (Reopened)

"You can get anything you want at Alice's Restaurant.
You can get anything you want at Alice's Restaurant.
Come right over in, it's around the back.
Just a half mile from the railroad track.
You can get anything you want at Alice's Restaurant.
Except Alice!"

Whatever you want you can find it here.
There's booze, cigarettes, food & even guns.
There's a blackboard menu that changes every day.
It's so exciting to see what's on today.
Today they are serving justice on a plate.
With it comes the best judges that money can buy.
Whatever your crime, you won't do any time.
If you have this meal, it's today's "special of the day"!

My favourite meals are the "Chef's Signature Dishes"!
There's "Hash cookies", so crunchy & light.
They are gluten free, sugar free & very healthy for you too.
His "Pièce de Résistance" is his "Magic Mushroom Stew".
Guaranteed to blow your mind.
It will take you higher than you've ever been before.
You'll be wanting to come for more & more & more.

If it's sex you're looking for, then look no more.
Alice has the best there is & that's for sure.
Their rates are high, $500 an hour.
It's a "GF experience" like no other.
You'll never regret it because you're getting the best.
Make sure to ask for the "Penthouse Suite", it has a glass roof.
You'll be floating in the stars, when you explode your load.
Just like a "Supernova" in the Heavens above.
You'll start to believe that you are in Lo♥e.

So, for whatever your needs, come on down.
Alice is open 24/7, 365 days, all year round.
Its doors are never closed but make sure to bring your money with you.
Because nothing's for free.
You can buy anything you want at Alice's Restaurant but make sure you bring your money with you.
You can buy anything you want at Alice's Restaurant come on over, everyone's welcome.
You can buy anything you want at Alice's Restaurant, excepting Alice!
You can buy anything you want at Alice's Restaurant, ok you but Alice too.
But it'll cost ya!
Alice doesn't come cheap, you hear!
You can buy anything you want at Alice's Restaurant, even Alice!

"The Don"
04.06.2020

Mindless

(less is better, less is more)

I am thoughtless.
I have no thoughts.
I am clueless.
I have no clues.
I am useless.
I am of no use.
I have no ideas.
I am idealess.
I am imagination-less.
I have no imagination.
I am sightless.
I have no sight.
I am fearless.
I have no fear.
I am sexless.
I have no sex.
I am genderless.
I have no gender.
I have no dick.
I am dick-less.
I have no friends.
I am friendless.
I have no sense.
I am senseless.
I have no principles.
I am principle-less.
I have no morality.
I am morality-less.
I have no scruples.
I am scruple-less.

I have no point.
I am pointless.
I no guts.
I am gutless.
I have no law.
I am lawless.
I have no bottom.
I am bottomless.
I have no end.
I am endless.
I have no fathom.
I am fathomless.
I have no voice.
I am voiceless.
I have no heart.
I am heartless.
I have no Humanity.
I am Humanity-less.
I have no self.
I am self-less.
I have no soul.
I am soulless.
I have no Lo♥e.
I am Lo♥e-less.
I have no brain.
I am brainless.
I have no mind.
I am mindless.

𝕸𝖎𝖓𝖉𝖑𝖊𝖘𝖘

(less is better, less is more)

"The Don"
05.06.2020

Mining Companies Care
(Oh, yes, they do, really!)

They love this great nation of ours.
It is true, they dig massive holes in the ground.
They destroy the environment.
They kill endangered species of fauna & flora.
They destroy pristine habits.
They dishonour sacred Aboriginal sites.
But let's not be too harsh on them.
They only have our best interests in mind.

They are building this great nation one hole at time.
Each new hole has to be bigger, wider & deeper than the last.
But don't worry, they believe in "regeneration".
Everything will back as it was before.
Even better than before!
Except the Aboriginal sacred site that was destroyed & can never be replaced.
It was an accident.
They blew up the wrong place.
They are deeply sorry for this mistake.
*"Please Elders, please accept our deepest heartfelt regret.
We will make sure it will NEVER happen again.
If it does, we will apologise again & again."*

Rio Tinto is a great friend of this beautiful land.
BHP is "The Big Australian".
There's Fortesque Metals owned by the great Australian entrepreneur, Andrew "Twiggy" Forrest.
A great friend of the Chinese as well.
And of course, who can forget the late mining magnate, Lang Hancock's daughter, Gina Rhinehart.
Great Aussie mining companies that ravage the land, digging for coal, iron ore & Uranium.

Don't worry that they are subsided by the Government with lower taxes & other benefits.
Don't worry that they hardly pay any taxes.
Don't worry that their profits go overseas.
Don't worry that they destroy the environment.
Don't worry that the permanently scare the land.
Don't worry that destroy sacred Aboriginal sites.
It's ok, they are making the country richer.
Exporting our great mineral reserves by digging it out of the ground.

"I love a sunburnt country,
A land of sweeping plains,
Of ragged mountain ranges,
Of droughts and flooding rains.
I love her far horizons,
I love her jewel-sea,
Her beauty and her terror –
The wide brown land for me!"

Mining Companies Care
(Oh, yes, they do, really!)

"The Don"
05.06.2020

This Land is Your Land
(Reconciliation)

The white man came it took it all.
The white man took with guns.
The white man killed them all.
The white man said there was nobody here.
The white man claimed this land for mother England.
The white man deemed it "Terra Nullis".

The white man brought diseases & vermin.
The white man brought religion to convert them.
The white man brought Christianity to teach them.
The white man brought GOD to this land.
The white man brought the Devil too.
The white man brought the end of the world.

The white man raped, tortured & killed.
The white man ravaged the land.
The white man introduced poison to this land.
The white man stole the children & took them away.
The white man destroyed their culture & their way of life.
The white man brought 200 years of pain, suffering & blood.
The white man has a lot to pay for.

There were many nations here when the white man arrived.
There were many Humans here when the white man set foot on this land.
The was a culture here that spanned 120,000 years into the past, when the white man opened fire.
There was "The Dreamtime", when the white man shot their guns.
There were sacred burial sites when the white man ravaged the land.
The children had families when the white man stole them & took them away.
There was spirituality, a connection between nature, the animals & the cosmos when the white introduced religion.

There was no God, when the white man came.
There was no Devil, before the white man came.
There was no need for them, when the white man came.
There were spirits of the river, the land & the sea, when white man came.
There was civilisation, law & order when the white man came.
The land was respected, when the white man came.
There was an understanding between the land & humans, when the white man came.

It's time for the white man to admit the truth.
It's time for the white man to come clean.
It's time for the white man to wash their hands.
It's time for the white wash the blood.
It's time for the white man admit their lies.
It's time for the white man to seek forgiveness.
It's time for the white man to give it back.

It's to time for the white man to set things right.
It's to time for the white man to make restitutions.
It's to time for the white man to pay reparations.
It's to time for the white man to do what's right.
It's to time for the white man to set the slate clean.
It's to time for the white man to bring back the Dreamtime".
It's time for the white man to rewrite "The Constitution!"

It's time for the white man to make amends.
It's time for the white man give it back.
It's time for the white man to "bend the knee".
It's time for the white man to pay for all the injustices of 200 years
It's time for the white man to ask for "Reconciliation".
It's time for the white man for to say, "This land is yours, here take it back!"
It's time for the white man for to say, "This land is your land" & that's a fact!

This Land is Your Land
(Reconciliation)

"The Don"
05.06.2020

The Masturbation Game
(Guess the Gender)

"The Masturbation Game" is a wholesome family game that everyone can play.
Play it at home with your whole family, including your children. It's very educational & is guaranteed to get everyone talking. A "massdebate" is sure to happen. Hours of fun for everyone! It's easy to play, just guess whether it's a female or a male that's masturbating.

Start "Masturbating" NOW!

(Masturbate responsibly!)

Wanking
Elabiaorating
Petting
Jerking off
Playing the clitar
Pulling oneself
Fingering
Ecstasizing
Spanking the monkey
Handjob
Frigging
Bliss-torising
Beating the meat
Shebopping
Playing with oneself
Hand relief
Self-gratification
Cruising for an oozing
Knob job
Toss-off
Stuffing your envelope
Flick the bean
Hand fuck

Jack-off
Mind the gap
Hand party.
Jerkin' the gherkin.
Klittra
Flying solo
Beating off
Jilling off
Polish the pearl
Flogging one's log
Petting the bunny.
Pleasuring oneself
Shooting off
Pushing your button
High Fiving
Spanking the stick
Tiggling
Punishing Percy
Servicing oneself
Getting rub burn
Petting the cat
Smacking Lester
Di-Yes
Strangling the snake
Petting the kitty.
Stroking one's salami
Willie & the hand jive
Orbiting Venus
Waxing the carrot
Buffing the muffin.
Whacking it
Fingerlifting
Poking fun
Yanking it.
Funtasizing
Milk your dick

Milking the mouse.
Choking the chicken
Doing a Meg Ryan
Jerking the Johnson
Bashing the Bishop
Strangling the goose
Pussitioning
Sperming the worm
Punching the munchkin
Lone Rangering
Punching the clown
Vibratizing
Slicking your stick
Pulling the pud
Singing Soprano
Skinning the onion.
Sap your wood
Plucking one's twanger
Killing a kitten
Rubbing the rigid rod
Pumping up the juice handle
Pleasure Cruising.
Procrastubating
Polishing one's knob.
Peeling the banana
Vajubilation
Peeling the wand
Pulling one's pud
Imaginactioning
Popping your cork
Checking your pulse
Painting the ceiling
Wet 'N' Wilding

"The Don"
06.06.2020

Cunt

(is not a dirty word)

It's the portal to this world.
It's the doorway that we all come through.
It's the exit from our first home.
It's the opening through which we are born.

It comes in all shapes & colours.
They are all different & unique.
Just like one's fingerprints, no one else has one like yours.
It's a beautiful part of your body.

Men are jealous of such a beautiful pussy.
They wish they had one instead of their ugly cock.
They Lo♥e it so much they have turn it around.
To mean Something ugly, disgusting & a complete piece of shit.

They've turned the cunt into a description of derision.
They've turned the word cunt into a description of hate.
They've turned the word cunt to describe an abomination.
They turned the cunt onto a description of hate.

Let's take the word back to describe what bit really is.
A cunt is a beautiful part of a woman's body.
A cunt is not an abomination.
A cunt is the portal of our birth.

Lo♥e the cunt.
I am a cunt.
You are a cunt.
Let's call everyone a cunt.

Call me a cunt.
A cunt is a badge of honour.
There is no greater accolade than to be called a cunt.
Because cunt is not a dirty word.

"The Don"
06.06.2020

World Environment Day
(6th June)

The 6th June is World Environment Day.
It's a good time to stop & take stock of the condition of our planet.
It's good to review what we have done & where we are at.
To see if we are either in the red or the black.

Global warming is accelerating at an ever-increasing rate.
The sea levels are rising faster than expected.
The ocean temperature is rising a couple of degrees Celsius each decade.
That's just the beginning, there's much more & I haven't even started yet.

The coral is dying in The Great Barrier Reef from the warmer water temperature.
They can't get no relief.
2019 was the hottest years since records began.
There were "mega" bushfires in Australia that could not be put out.

They destroyed thousands of hectares of flora & fauna.
Destroying the habits of endangered species.
Like the beautiful koala, that does no harm to anyone.
They are now endangered to become extinct if this trend continues on.

Weather patterns have become unpredictable & severe.
Causing massive flooding, heat waves, wind storms, cyclones.
Even computer modelling cannot keep with unpredictable changes.
There are no longer four seasons like it was in the past.

Summer, winter, spring & autumn no longer are separate & distinct.
Everything is merging into one big soup.
The animals & the plants they recognise this confusion.
They don't what do either, whether to be dormant or awake.

The Arctic & Antarctic ice is melting.
The ocean is rising.
The permafrost is Siberia is melting.
The face of the planet is changing forever.

The Amazon, the lungs of the planet.
Are being cut down & burnt.
The jungles of Indonesia are being cut down.
The Great Apes & the Orangutans are losing their homes.

So, the outcome for our planet is looking very bleak.
Politicians cannot be trusted because they are to blame.
It's their decisions that have created this situation.
We must get rid of them quickly or there will be continued devastation.

We must elect people into power that put the environment first.
Not money, profits or selfish power pursuits.
People with ideals, integrity & principles.
People who cannot be bought by vested interests.

People who are strong & committed to this struggle.
Because the exploitation of the environment is a powerful force.
They will be up against very powerful opponents.
The mining companies, the banks & huge multinational corporations all have vested interests.

All they care about is the all mighty dollar.
Profits are all they care about.
The destruction of the environment is just a price one must pay.
The extinction of thousands of species of fawn, flora & ancient,
Aboriginal, heritage, sacred burial sites are just collateral damage.

Now is the time to stop & say,
"It's time for action, join us or get out of our way.
We have no time to lose.
Time is running out.
If we want a habitable planet for our children to live on".

World Environment Day
(6th June)

"The Don"
06.06.2020
(World Environment Day)

Taking it to the Streets

You got something to say?
You got something to protest about?
You see things that you don't like.
You see injustices & exploitation about.
You wanna express your rage.
You wanna express your disgust.
What can you do about it?
What can you do let it all out?
You can take it to the streets.

Let's organise a protest.
Let's organise a march.
Let's organise a rally.
Let's show our rage.
Let's get together.
There's power in numbers.
Let's show them what we think.
Let's show what we feel.
Let's it take it to the streets.

Let's make raise our placards high.
Let's fly our banners in the wind.
Let's shout our message to the rooftops.
And then even higher again.
Let's sing or songs of change to the heavens.
Let's raise our arms in defiance.
Let's dance to the rhythm of life.
Let's tell them that this is not the way things should be.
Let's in our thousands meet & take to the streets.

Let's show them that this is the voice of the people.
Let's tell them we want changes.
Let's show that we cannot be stopped.
Let's show that we will march even if we break the law.
Let's show all that this a basic human right.
To express our voice against the powers of oppression & might.
That don't need permission or a permit to express our fundamental right.
This is democracy not a dictatorship, a Fascist or Police State.
We're taking it to the streets & we're not looking for a fight.

We're taking it to the streets, this is our fundamental democratic right.
We're taking it to the streets, we'll break the law because we know we're right.
We're taking it to the streets, we're not looking for a fight.
We're taking to the streets, to show everyone our might.
We're taking to the streets, so join us if you agree with our plight.
We're taking to the streets, because we wanna be in sight.
We're taking it to the streets, so comewith us & fly a kite.
We're taking it to the streets because it's right, it's right, it's right!

"The Don"
06.06.2020

Recurring Dream

I have this recurring dream.
Night after night.
What does it mean?
I am back at school.
In an English class.
We are studying Shakespeare.
One of his plays.
But I haven't been paying attention.
I don't have all the notes.
I can't even remember the name of the play.
All I can remember is that is it's *"A Midsummer's Something or Other"*.

I am in the classroom with my old friend Greg.
The teacher is there, *Mr Hosford*.
We are probably in Year 12 of High School.
I explain him the situation & ask him for help.
He tells me the story.
It's about this aristocratic family.
That live in a big old mansion.
The Lord of the mansion is in a catatonic state.
I ask if he's dead.
He just sits in his armchair like a vegetable.
He's neither dead or alive.

There's character called *"Gerherty"*.
He's their family lawyer.
He's looking into the family's legal affairs.
There are complications with the Estate.
Their financial situation is becoming desperate.
It is caught up in trusts & bonds without any income.
As is always the case with the rich & the wealthy.
They never want to pay there far share.
To try to get away with paying as little as taxes as possible.
Gerherty has been instructed to sort out this complicated & messy situation.

There is tension in the mansion.
The *"Lady of the Manor"* is in deep distress.
She is concerned about the future.
She's concerned about what happen to their lifestyle.
She is concerned about what her neighbours will think.
She is concerned about her friends & what a bad look it will be.
To lose everything.

If only the *"Lord of the Manor"* had set up things right.
She wouldn't be in this dreadful plight.
If only he'd hadn't been so selfish, before he had his *"turn"*.
She wouldn't be in this mess.
He is now just a blubbering idiot that has to be fed by a servant.
"This is how we end up", she thinks to herself.
"Well, it's not going to happen to me", she states to herself.

Then, I awake from this recurring dream.
I have it quite often & I lay in bed & wonder.
"What the fuck does this all mean?"

Recurring Dream

"The Don"
07.06.2020

Respect

Respect is a two-way thing.
Respect is how you treat others.
Respect is about valuing others.
Respect is about not putting yourself above someone else.
Respect is about valuing everyone as equals.
Respect is about treating everyone the same.
Respect is about not putting others down
Respect is about dignity.
Respect also has to do with oneself.
Respect is also to respect oneself.
Respect yourself, don't put yourself down.
Respect others just like you respect yourself.
Respect is our bond.
Respect is what ties us together.
Respect others, no matter the situation.
Respect is a fundamental human right.
Respect is only given, if you deserve it.
Respect is returned the same way.
Respect is returned when you deserve it, because of the things you do & say.
Respect is what Aretha Franklin sang about, so long ago.

"All I'm askin'
Is for a little respect when you get home (just a little bit)
Hey baby (just a little bit) when you get home
(Just a little bit) mister (just a little bit)."

"R-E-S-P-E-C-T
Find out what it means to me
R-E-S-P-E-C-T
Take care, TCB
Oh (sock it to me, sock it to me, sock it to me, sock it to me)
A little respect (sock it to me, sock it to me, sock it to me, sock it to me)
Whoa, babe (just a little bit)
A little respect (just a little bit)
I get tired (just a little bit)
Keep on tryin' (just a little bit)."

"The Don"
07.06.2020

Metamorphosis

Metamorphosis has got you.
It's got you by the head.

Metamorphosis has got you.
It's pretty soon we're gonna be Dead.

Metamorphosis has got you.
It's got you by the balls.

Metamorphosis has got you.
It's got you outta bed.

Metamorphosis has got you.
It's got you by your throat.

Metamorphosis has got you.
It's about to rock your boat.

Metamorphosis has got you.
It's got you by your pussy.

Metamorphosis has got you.
It doesn't care, it's not fussy.

Metamorphosis has got you.
It's got you by your "short & curlies".

Metamorphosis has got you.
It even takes little girlies.

Metamorphosis has got you.
It's got you to your knees.

Metamorphosis has got you.
It doesn't do it by degrees.

Metamorphosis has got you.
It's got inside you veins.

Metamorphosis has got you.
It's your loss & it's gains.

Metamorphosis has got you.
It will never let you go.

Metamorphosis s has got you.
It'll do you nice & slow.

Metamorphosis has got you.
It's not gonna let you run away.

Metamorphosis has got you.
It's not gonna let you have a say.

Metamorphosis has got you.
It's got you on the ground.

Metamorphosis has got you.
It'll make sure you'll never be found.

Metamorphosis has got you.
It's not gonna make you wake up one morning.

Metamorphosis has got you.
It'll be your end & there'll be no new day dawning.

Metamorphosis

has got you.

"The Don"
07.06.2020

Yes, That's Me Babe
(That's Me You're Looking for Babe)

Don't look away from my window.
You don't need to leave as agreed.
I'm the one you want, babe.
I'm the one you need.

You say you're searchin' for someone.
Who's always strong & never weak.
To defend you & protect you.
Whether you are wrong or right.
Someone to do all this & maybe more.
Yes, that's me, babe.
Yes, yes, yes, yes that's me, babe.
That's me you're lookin' for, babe.

I'm the one you want, babe.
I will not let you down.

You say you're need someone
Who will be there when you call?
Someone to keep an on you.
Someone in case you fall.
Someone who will a friend to you and maybe more.
Yes, that's me, babe.
Yes, yes, yes, yes that's me, babe.
That's me you're lookin' for, babe.

You say you need someone.
Who you can call, each time you fall,
To give you flowers now then.
And to be there when you call
A friend, a lover & baby that's all.
Yes, that's me, babe.
Yes, yes, yes, yes that's me, babe.
That's me you're lookin' for, babe.

You say you want someone.
Who will always have your back for you,
To make sure that everything's alright.
To check on you that's all.
Someone on a cold & rainy night.
Yes, that's me, babe.
Yes, yes, yes, yes, that's me, babe.
That's me you're lookin' for, babe.

Thanks to B. Dylan

"The Don"
07.06.2020

Police Brutality

Why?
You ask.
Why do police use excessive force?
You ask.
Is it the protesters' fault?
You ask.
Are they to blame?
You ask.
Why do they incite violence?
You ask.
Why don't they protest in other ways?
You ask.
Why do they have to protest on the streets?
You ask.
Why do they have to shout & yell?
You ask.
Why do they have to carry banners & signs?
You ask.
Why can't they use social media?
You ask.
Why don't they obey the law?
You ask.

Why does the government want to ban them?
You ask.
Why does the police have to use riot shields?
You ask.
Why does the police have to be in such large numbers?
You ask.
Why does the police have to be on horses?
You ask.
Why does the police report have to use capsicum spray?
You ask.
Why does the police have to be so aggressive?
You ask.
Why does the police have to be so rough?
You ask?
Why does the police have to use brute force?
You ask.
Why does the police have to be violent?
You ask.

Why is it always this way?
You ask.
Why does history keep repeating itself?
You ask.
Why is it that police have always acted with brutality?
You ask.
Why is it that governments are scared of letting people have their say?
You ask.
Why is that we need permission to march in the streets?
You ask.
Why is that people have to struggle to voice their objections?
You ask.
Why is that they have to struggle against injustices?
You ask.

Why is it those in power live in so much fear?
You ask.
Why they are so strongly defending their positions even though they know it is wrong?
You ask.
Why they so determined not to let people express themselves in a collective way?
You ask.
Why don't they rejoice when 50,000 or more people take to the streets?
You ask.
Why don't they say, "Wow, that's fantastic to see!"?
You ask.
Why don't they proclaim, "This is the voice of the people!"?
You ask.
Why do they instead, want to stop this from spreading?
You ask.
Why do they, instead want to kill it dead?
You ask.
Why do they introduce even more laws & harsher penalties?
You ask.
Why do they want to punish people for speaking out?
You ask.
Why do they want to stop people from taking things into their own hands?
You ask.
Why?
Why?
Why?
Oh, why?

"The Don"
07.06.2020

Be Weird

(don't be NORMAL)

Be different.
Be unusual.
Be eccentric.
Be irreverent.
Be funny.
Be crazy.
Be mad.
Be madcap.
Be a looney.
Be zany.
Be abnormal.
Be strange.
Be mysterious.,
Be a free thinker.
Be curious.
Be artistic.
Be creative.
Be self-aware
Be caring.
Be respectful.
Be compassionate.
Be friendly.
Be focused.
Be worldly.
Be wordy.

Be emotional.
Be kind.
Be social.
Be Lo♥ing.
Be nurturing.
Be a student.
Be a teacher.
Be musical.
Be a thinker.
Be a traveller.
Be interesting.
Be interested.
Be way-out.
Be outlandish.
Be unorthodox.
Be unconventional.
Be anti-establishment.
Be an adventurer.
Be an INDIVIDUAL.
Be HUMAN.
Be YOURSELF.
Be WEIRD.
But DON'T be NORMAL!

"The Don"
08.06.2020

"The Don" Will Fuck You
(& educate you at the same time)

"The Don" will fuck you (& educate you at the same time).
How long does it take the light from the Sun to reach the Earth!
8 minutes.

"The Don" will fuck you (& educate you at the same time).
What is Bob Dylan's birth name?
Robert Zimmerman.

"The Don" will fuck you (& educate you at the same time).
What date was the first atomic bomb dropped on the Japanese city of Hiroshima?
6th August 1945.

"The Don" will fuck you (& educate you at the same time).
What is the speed of sound?
330 metres per second.

"The Don" will fuck you (& educate you at the same time).
Who led the "Manhattan Project" that developed the first atomic bomb?
Robert Oppenheimer.

"The Don" will fuck you (& educate you at the same time).
When did Neil Armstrong land on the Moon?
19th July 1969.

"The Don" will fuck you (& educate you at the same time).
What is the piece of skin between a woman's pussy & her arse called?
The perineum.

"The Don" will fuck you (& educate you at the same time).
Who said "The world is a stage & we are all but actors on it"?
William Shakespeare.

"The Don" will fuck you (& educate you at the same time).
What is Einstein's famous equation that relates Energy & Matter?
E=mc*2.

"The Don" will fuck you (& educate you at the same time).
Where was the singer Tom Jones born?
Pontypridd, Wales.

"The Don" will fuck you (& educate you at the same time).
In what year did Captain Cook shoot the first Aboriginal?
1770.

"The Don" will fuck you (& educate you at the same time).
What is a binary number?
A number that is made up of only ones & zeros.

"The Don" will fuck you (& educate you at the same time).
What is the scientific term for fucking?
Fornication.

"The Don" will fuck you (& educate you at the same time).
Who was the first Prime Minister of Australia?
Sir Edmond Barton.

"The Don" will fuck you (& educate you at the same time).
Who wrote & sang "Walk on The Wild Side"?
Lou Reed.

"The Don" will fuck you (& educate you at the same time).
What is the scientific word for "shit"?
Faeces.

"The Don" will fuck you (& educate you at the same time).
Who wrote the novel "Frankenstein"?
Mary Shelley.

"The Don" will fuck you (& educate you at the same time).
What is the chemical process in plants that converts light into food?
Photosynthesis.

"The Don" will fuck you (& educate you at the same time).
What is the classic MkII lineup of Deep Purple?
Richie Blackmore, Jon Lord, Ian Gillan, Roger Glover & Ian Piace.

"The Don" will fuck you (& educate you at the same time).
What family of animals do worms belong to?
Nematodes.

"The Don" will fuck you (& educate you at the same time).
Where & when was Bob Dylan born?
Duluth, Minnesota, USA, 24th May 1941

"The Don" will fuck you (& educate you at the same time).
Which artist is credited for beginning the "Cubist" movement in art?
Pablo Picasso.

"The Don"
08.06.2020

Living in a Fantasy World

I live in my imagination.
I live in my mind.
I live in a world of make believe.
I live in a world of illusion.
I live in a world of my own making.
I live in a fantasy world.

It's my own world that I live in.
A world where I can do whatever I like.
A world where I make up my own rules & regulations.
A world where I am always the hero.
A world where I always get the girl.

A world in which,
I can do whatever I want.
I can say whatever I want.
I can think whatever I want.
I can fuck whomever I want.
It's my world & no one can tell me what to do.

I live in a fantasy world.
I fantasy world created by me.
A fantasy world that no one else can see.
A fantasy world that's for free.
A fantasy world of "make-believe".
A fantasy world just for.

I lo♥e my fantasy world.
Do you lo♥e YOUR fantasy world as much as I lo♥e mine?

"The Don"
08.06.2020

Violence

Violence is everywhere.
We live in a violent world.
Violence is sometimes hard to see.
We are all violent.
Yep, even you & me.

Violence is in the way we think.
It's in our society.
Violence is in the way we feel.
It's in our families.
Violence is in our values.

Violence is in the System.
It's in our heads.
Violence is the Economy.
It's in our education.
Violence is taught to us.

Violence is physical.
Violence is psychological.
Violence is economic.
Violence is discrimination.
Violence is encouraged in Society.

Violence does not solve problems.
It in fact causes conflicts.
Violence has never stopped wars.
It in fact causes wars.
Violence is not the solution.

Violence is about "Power".
Violence is about "Abuse".
Violence is about "Aggression".
Violence is about "Domination".
Violence is about "Exploitation".

Violence can be unlearned.
Violence can be untaught.
Violence can be eliminated.
Violence can be removed.
Violence can become *"NON-VIOLENCE"*!

"The Don"
08.06.2020

History Repeats

We are enchained to the Past.
We are prisoners of our past actions.
We are captives to what we have done before.
Because our history repeats.

We are bound by what we have done before.
We can already foretell our Future.
We are bound by the Past.
Our Future is our past because history repeats.

We are our past actions.
We have no choice about it.
We are doomed to repeat our mistakes.
Our past is always present because history repeats.

We are our past behaviours.
We are our past thoughts.
We will keep repeating things over & over again.
Our Future is already determined because history repeats.

We have no choice about it.
We haven't got a say.
We are doomed to repeat our past failures.
No matter what we do or say because history repeats.

We think that we are free.
We think that we make our decisions.
We think that we can make our Future.
But this is just bullshit because history repeats.

We are just pawns to our Past.
We are completely determined by what we have done before.
We can call it Fate, destiny or conditioned behaviour.
It doesn't matter because history repeats.

We are destined to repeat mistakes.
We tethered to our past actions.
We are captured by its invisible web.
In its embrace, its dance called Life, because history ALWAYS repeats.

"The Don"
09.06.2020

The White Devil

They stood on the shoreline.
They watched in amazement.
They had never seen anything like this before.
They were spirits sent by the Gods.
They were wrong.
The White Devil had arrived.

They heard a noise pierce their ears.
They heard a noise sharp as thunder in the sky.
They saw a puff of smoke far off shore.
They saw one of their brothers fall to the ground.
The White Devil had spoken.

They saw blood coming out from his body.
They saw their brother on the ground dying.
They were scared & started to scatter.
They quickly realised that these were not friendly Gods.
The White Devil had powerful, evil magic that could kill them from a distance.

They ran into the bushes to hid.
They saw huge objects reach the shore.
They saw strange white beings getting off.
They were wearing strange things on their bodies & their heads.
The White Devil had arrived & set foot upon their land.

They knew that theses strangers were a threat.
They knew that these white beings were evil.
They were scared of these white beings.
They were scared because they had seen the powerful magic that they held.
The White Devil had arrived with the magic stick.

They felt the power of "The White Devil's" magic stick.
They heard its noise,
They saw its puff of smoke
They saw far away a brother or sister fall to the ground bleeding, dead or dying.
The White Devil held the power of the magic stick in his hand.

They knew then that they were no match.
They knew then that the Devil had arrived.
They knew then that their world would never be the same again.
They knew then that their world had died.
The White Devil had arrived & their world would never be the same again.

"The Don"
09.06.2020

Power to the People

(with thanks to J. Lennon)

You say you want a revolution.
Well you know that it's in our hands.
You say you want to change the constitution.
We you know we can make demands.

But when we choose leaders that do what we want.
When choose leaders don't do what we say.
When our leaders just turn away.
We say, Power to the People.

You know we have the power.
The power is in our hands.
They must do what we say.
They can't get away.

We sing......
Power to the People!
Power to the People!
Power to the People!
Power to the People right on!

People have the power.
People have the strength.
People can change the Future.
Because Power to the People right on.

You say you don't like our leaders.
You are angry that they don't give a shit.
Well don't just sit in your hands, let's do something about.
Because people have the power in their hands.

Come on let's sing.
Power to the People.
Power to the People.
Power to the People right on.

Raise your voices higher.
Power to the People.
Power to the People.
Power to the People it's on!

You say you want a revolution.
Well, we've got one here right now.
There's nothing left to say.
We're not goin' away.
We're here to stay.
No matter how long it takes.
Where gonna stay until you break.
And we know that you will.
Because you're as weak as piss.
And that right is on our side.
And that might, is not right.
And that we'll win fight.
Because we're gonna stay here all day & all night.
And we'll win the day.
There's nothing you can do or say.
We won't bow down.
To your threats or your fears.
We have lasted this long.
We've shed all our tears.
Because we are all one.
All for one & one for all.
One giant voice.
That sings in glorious harmony.

Sing it!
Power to the People
Power to the People.
Power to the People right on.

Louder!
Power to the People.
Power to the People.
Power to the People it's on!

"The Don"
09.06.2020

Fuck the Patriarchy!

(with thanks to M. Pringle)

Fuck the male dominated society.
Fuck the male chauvinist pigs.
Fuck the male arsehole politicians.
Fuck the male fascist police.
Fuck the male dominated establishment.
Fuck the male CEOs of heads of industry.
Fuck the Patriarchy!

Patriarchy is endemic in our society.
Patriarchy is embedded into the fabric of our lives.
Patriarchy is all about male control.
Patriarchy is all about male domination.
Patriarchy is all about power.
Patriarchy is all about the "Cock".
Fuck the Patriarchy!

It's time for Patriarchy to be dismantled.
It's time for Patriarchy to be brought down.
It's time for Patriarchy to be buried once & for all.
It's time for Patriarchy to be put underground.
It's time for Patriarchy to be put to the sword.
It's time for Patriarchy to be put to rest.
It's time to fuck the Patriarchy!

It's time for Matriarchy to arise.
It's time for Matriarchy to take control.
It's time for Matriarchy to bring us out of the darkness.
It's time for Matriarchy to shine its light.
It's time for Matriarchy to put its foot down.
It's time for Matriarchy to fuck the Patriarchy.

"The Don"
09.06.2020

"Fuck the Patriarchy"
By Mariclaire Pringle

Lightning Source UK Ltd.
Milton Keynes UK
UKHW050719141020
371538UK00004B/101